GRAPHIC EXPEDITIONS

The SECRETS of MARTIAL ARTS

AN *Isabel Soto* INVESTIGATION

Christopher Harbo

illustrated by Joe Staton and Al Milgrom

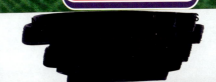

www.raintreepublishers.co.uk
Visit our website to find out
more information about
Raintree books.

To order:
☎ Phone 0845 6044371
🖨 Fax +44 (0) 1865 312263
✉ Email myorders@raintreepublishers.co.uk

Customers from outside the UK please telephone +44 1865 312262

Raintree is an imprint of Capstone Global Library Limited, a company incorporated in England and
Wales having its registered office at 7 Pilgrim Street, London EC4V 6LB
Registered company number: 6695882

Text © Capstone Press 2010
First published by Capstone Press in 2010
First published in hardback in the United Kingdom by Capstone Global Library Ltd in 2011
First published in paperback in the United Kingdom by Capstone Global Library Ltd in 2012
The moral rights of the proprietor have been asserted.

British Library Cataloguing in Publication Data
Harbo, Christopher – Secrets of martial arts: an Isabel Soto investigation
A full catalogue record for this book is available from the British Library.

ISBN 978 1 406 21815 2 (hardback)   ISBN 978 1 406 22163 3 (paperback)
14 13 12 11 10   15 14 13 12 11
10 9 8 7 6 5 4 3 2 1   10 9 8 7 6 5 4 3 2 1

Designer: Alison Thiele
Cover artist: Tod Smith
Colourist: Michael Kelleher
Media researcher: Wanda Winch
UK Editor: Diyan Leake
Originated by Capstone Global Library Ltd
Printed and bound in China by South China Printing Company Limited

Disclaimer
All the Internet addresses (URLs) given in this book were valid at the time of going to press.
However, due to the dynamic nature of the Internet, some addresses may have changed, or sites may
have changed or ceased to exist since publication. While the publisher regrets any inconvenience this
may cause readers, no responsibility for any such changes can be accepted by the publisher.

Photo credits:
Capstone Studio/Karon Dubke, 11, 13, 23

Design elements:
Shutterstock/Chen Ping Hung (framed edge design);
Mushakesa (abstract lines design); Najin (old pa

CONTENTS

BZZZT! BZZZT!

Rats! I'm running late for my martial arts training!

MARTIAL ARTS LESSON

ROOOAAAR!

I'd better hurry.

Master Adachi doesn't like it when I'm late.

Adachi Training Hall, Osaka, Japan, present day

That should be easy. Many books have —

Not so fast, Miss Isabel. Your path does not run through the library.

You will gain knowledge of martial arts by searching for the shadowless kick.

Is that a karate move?

That is what you must discover.

Search for the shadowless kick. Your knowledge of martial arts will bloom along the way.

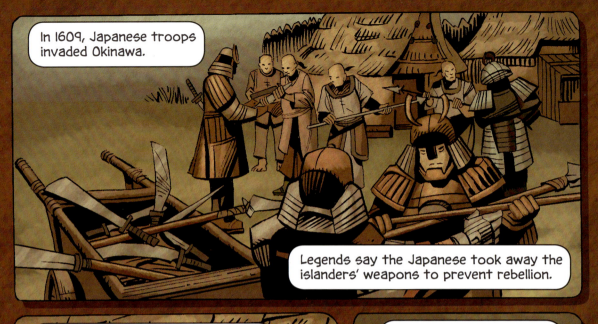

In 1609, Japanese troops invaded Okinawa.

Legends say the Japanese took away the islanders' weapons to prevent rebellion.

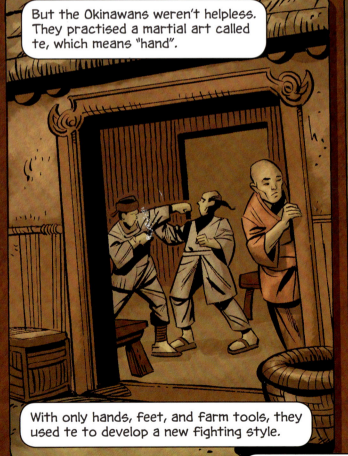

But the Okinawans weren't helpless. They practised a martial art called te, which means "hand".

With only hands, feet, and farm tools, they used te to develop a new fighting style.

With it, they could defeat armed enemies . . .

. . . with single, powerful strikes.

HIIIYAHHH!

Today power remains a key to karate.

Students use their hands, feet, knees, and elbows to knock down opponents with powerful blows.

That reminds me. Do you know a move called the shadowless kick?

Karate has many kicks, but the shadowless kick isn't one of them.

Perhaps you should look into jujitsu. It was practised by Japan's samurai warriors.

Thanks, Oda Sensei. I'll see if the samurai have the answer I need.

KARATE KATA

Karate students practise kata as part of their training. A kata is a series of blocks, punches, and kicks against an imaginary attacker. Students work hard to perform kata perfectly. Kata teach students to focus and move their bodies with control.

In that case, I'm glad you're a skilled warrior. I've heard the samurai practise jujitsu.

That's true. My jujitsu training started at a very early age.

Am I correct that jujitsu means the "art of flexibility" in Japanese?

Yes. It's a martial art with countermoves for every attack. Jujitsu is full of throws, arm locks, pins, and bone-breaking moves.

JUDO

Judo wouldn't exist without jujitsu. In 1882, Dr Jigoro Kano set up a school to teach judo, based on the best skills and practices he learned from jujitsu. Today judo is a popular sport worldwide, famous for its powerful throwing and wrestling moves. It has been an Olympic sport since 1964.

Over the years, new fighting styles developed that used both punching and kicking.

In 1910, Japan took control of Korea. For the next 35 years, the Japanese banned all Korean martial arts.

But some people practised in secret. When the Japanese finally left, Korean martial arts bloomed again.

In 1955, martial arts schools throughout Korea met to form one Korean martial art.

From this meeting, modern tae kwon do was born.

Courtesy means always being respectful.

Integrity means being honest with yourself and everyone.

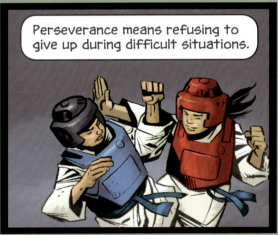

Perseverance means refusing to give up during difficult situations.

Self-control means controlling your body and mind and taking responsibility for your actions.

Indomitable spirit means having great courage and refusing to be controlled by another.

Only then will you be able to break the boards.

CRACK!

Tae kwon do kicks are impressive. Have you ever heard of the shadowless kick?

I'm afraid you won't find the shadowless kick in tae kwon do.

But you might have luck with the Chinese martial art of kung fu.

Thanks for the tip! I'll head to China next.

A BRITISH TAE KWON DO CHAMPION

Tae kwon do was introduced into the United Kingdom in 1967 but it took nearly 35 years to produce a British world champion. Sarah Stevenson became the first British tae kwon do champion at the World Championships in 2001. She won a bronze medal at the 2008 Olympic Games in Beijing, China.

Buddhist temple, China, present day

YAAAA!

HAAAA!

Whoa!

Please accept our apology, Miss.

That's OK. I'm glad I bumped into you. Could you share some of kung fu's history with me?

Certainly. According to legend, kung fu began more than 1,500 years ago.

Bodhidharma, a Buddhist monk from India, visited China's Shaolin Temple.

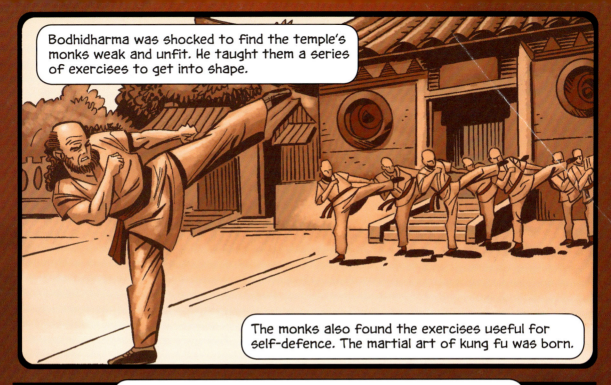

Bodhidharma was shocked to find the temple's monks weak and unfit. He taught them a series of exercises to get into shape.

The monks also found the exercises useful for self-defence. The martial art of kung fu was born.

Since Bodhidharma's time, kung fu has developed many styles.

TIGER STYLE

CRANE STYLE

SNAKE STYLE

PRAYING MANTIS STYLE

Some styles copy the movements of animals.

NORTHERN AND SOUTHERN KUNG FU

Kung fu styles are often divided into northern and southern styles. Northern kung fu styles use high, powerful kicks and jumps and smooth, fast moves. Southern styles use strong arm and hand techniques, low kicks, and stable positions.

Adachi Training Hall, Osaka, Japan, present day

I'm back, Master Adachi.

Hello, Miss Isabel. How was your journey?

I had an amazing trip! I understand karate, jujitsu, tae kwon do, and kung fu much better now.

Each martial art has a different history. But they all are powerful fighting and self-defence styles.

And martial arts are about more than just strength. They all draw on a strong mental focus to truly master their techniques.

26

MORE ABOUT
MARTIAL ARTS

The shadowless kick is a lightning-fast kick that is launched while an opponent is busy blocking multiple, swift punches. Chinese folk hero Wong Fei Hung is famous for his skill with this technique. Legends about his life and adventures have been made into many movies.

Jujitsu was first made popular in the United Kingdom when a Japanese instructor named Yukio Tani came to London in 1900. Tani gave jujitsu demonstrations in theatres, accepting challenges from people in the audience.

Crouching Tiger, Hidden Dragon (2000) is a Chinese martial arts and wuxia film. The heroes in wuxia stories are bound by a code that requires them to use their skills to right wrongs, especially when the helpless are oppressed. *Crouching Tiger, Hidden Dragon* won many awards and inspired a number of further martial arts films.

Karate means "empty hand", but the martial art includes some weapons. Because the Japanese banned all weapons, the Okinawans turned to farming tools to defend themselves. The kama is a karate weapon based on a tool used to harvest rice. It has a curved blade with a short wooden handle. Some karate schools still practice techniques with the kama.

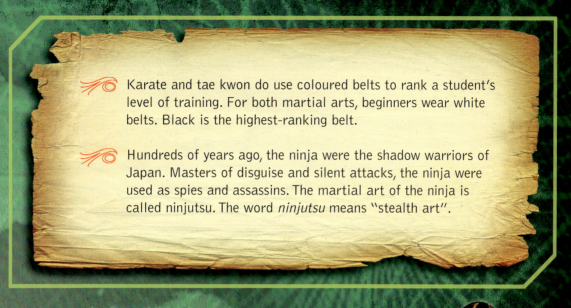

Karate and tae kwon do use coloured belts to rank a student's level of training. For both martial arts, beginners wear white belts. Black is the highest-ranking belt.

Hundreds of years ago, the ninja were the shadow warriors of Japan. Masters of disguise and silent attacks, the ninja were used as spies and assassins. The martial art of the ninja is called ninjutsu. The word *ninjutsu* means "stealth art".

MORE ABOUT

Isabel Soto

NAME: Isabel "Izzy" Soto
INTERESTS: People and places
BUILD: Athletic **HAIR:** Dark Brown
EYES: Brown **HEIGHT:** 1.70 m

WISP: The Worldwide Inter-dimensional Space/Time Portal developed by Max Axiom at Axiom Laboratory.

BACKSTORY: Isabel "Izzy" Soto caught the humanities bug as a little girl. Every night, her grandfather told her about his adventures exploring ancient ruins in South America. He believed people can learn a lot from other cultures and places.

Izzy's interest in cultures followed her through school and beyond. She studied history and geography. On one research trip, she discovered an ancient stone with mysterious energy. Izzy took the stone to Super Scientist Max Axiom, who determined that the stone's energy cuts across space and time. Harnessing the power of the stone, he built a device called the WISP. It opens windows to any place and any time. Although she must not use the WISP to change history, Izzy now explores events wherever and whenever they happen, solving a few mysteries along the way.

GLOSSARY

assassin person who murders a well-known or important person, such as a president

bandit armed robber, usually a member of a gang

combat fight between people or armies

confidence strong belief in your own abilities

countermove a move or other action made in response to a move made by an opponent

dojo Japanese word for a karate training hall. *Dojo* actually means "the place where the way is revealed".

flexibility ability to change quickly in response to changing situations or conditions

indomitable impossible to dominate or defeat

kata series of positions and movements used in the practice of martial arts

opponent person who competes against another person in a fight or contest

rebellion armed fight against the government or people in charge

sensei Japanese word for "teacher"

spar practise fighting

tenet principle or belief held in common by members of an organization, movement, or profession

FIND OUT MORE

BOOKS

Taekwondo Kids, Volker Dornemann (Meyer & Meyer, 2008)

The Kids' Karate Workbook: A Take-Home Training Guide for Young Martial Artists, Didi Goodman (Blue Snake, 2009)

A World Class Judo Champion (Making of a Champion series), Paul Mason (Heinemann Library, 2005)

WEBSITES

news.bbc.co.uk/sport2/hi/olympics/taekwondo/7301041.stm
Check out Olympic silver-medallist Sarah Stevenson's video guide to tae kwon do.

news.bbc.co.uk/sport2/hi/olympics/judo/7416923.stm
Learn some basic principles for becoming a great judoka with Team GB's Euan Burton and Craig Fallon.

martialartsclubs.co.uk/index.aspx
This website provides a directory of martial arts clubs and classes throughout the United Kingdom.

NDEX